BEING ATTENTION

Jean-Claude Lubtchansky

BEING ATTENTION

Meetings with a Gurdjieff Guide
in Provence, Holland, and New York

Fran Shaw

Indications Press
New York

www.franshawbooks.com

Author's Note: All of these informal talks (Parts One, Two, and Three of this book) are my best recollection of what Jean-Claude Lubtchansky said when I had the opportunity to hear him speak at particular times and places (2007-2018). In these fragments, written down immediately after those meetings, I have tried to bring his exact wording. Please note that English was a second language for him and the material quoted here is faithful to his expression, never paraphrased, in hopes of conveying its vibrational quality.

All quotations from Michel de Salzmann are from *The Next Attention (Notes on The Next Attention)*. His son Alexandre de Salzmann's quotation that begins Part Two is from the *Gurdjieff International Review*, Vol. XIII (2). Jean-Claude Lubtchansky's quotation that begins the Appendix is from *The Pandemic Years, 2020-2022*, p. 30.

Book design by Yuko Uchikawa
Photographic portrait courtesy of Carole Lubtchansky

With heartfelt thanks to Aubrey Paull, Sue Kagan, Lillian Firestone, David Shaw, Michel de Salzmann, Alexandre de Salzmann, Carole Lubtchansky and the Lubtchansky family.

ISBN 979-8-9857642-3-9

Library of Congress Control Number: 2024930442

Gently, gently, open. More and more.
Return to silent mind and this Light in you.
Like the statues on Easter Island: just receive.

—Jean-Claude Lubtchansky

*For Jean-Claude
and all of his companions*

CONTENTS

APPENDIX

CODA

PREFACE

Being Attention:
Working with Jean-Claude

We are at the beginning of a process.
To be aware of a current.... When I dwell
in the awareness, unidentified with
the contents of awareness, I am in the
stillness which is always there... truly
magical. It is an inner shift.... All that is
required is a kind of remembering to
bring it about, and then watchfulness
against being distracted.... Dwelling in
stillness is the channel through which the
other current can flow. It *is* the current.

—Jean-Claude Lubtchansky

There is a secret road that winds around Roman ruins outside a village in the South of France. It's Van Gogh country—but where are the heavenly fields lavendering? Here mostly scrub bush and olive trees. Arid sun. A long driveway that keeps going, even past our destination: the summer estate of French filmmaker Jean-Claude Lubtchansky. The constant hum of cicadas heightens the stillness.

Pay the taxi driver. Sit on a bench in the garden where refreshments await dedicated practitioners of the Work brought by G. I. Gurdjieff for awakening in the midst of everyday life. The word *work* for us means active attention, free from all my concerns, and subtle enough, perhaps, to join for a moment the Intelligence of the cosmos. Seeing objectively, being present, related to higher energies—all these are prominent themes.

What prompts my coming to this week-long retreat is a manuscript-in-progress, drawn from my journals, of Dr. Michel de Salzmann's talks. From 1990 to 2001, Michel (as he preferred to be called) guided the Gurdjieff Work worldwide. With his passing, his *confrère* Jean-Claude (as he preferred to be called) took on that role. It would not feel right to publish the book without his support.

Is Jean-Claude here in the garden? Not sure, having seen him only once before, fourteen years earlier at a Work retreat in the alpine village of Chandolin, Switzerland. Ninety of us, newly arrived from around the world, await dinner in the dining hall looking onto the peaks. We sit in rows facing the head table of elders in the Work, with Michel at the center. To his right, so it is said, is Jean-Claude.

First impression: Michel and Jean-Claude, their heads together, joking with each other—having a fine time—while the rest of us sit as stone-faced as the statues of Easter Island. More surprises. During a discussion about efforts to awaken, Jean-Claude says bluntly, "The only role the mind has to play is to leave the room." And as one listens to Michel's voice, every time he speaks of what he calls "this other Attention," a shift occurs. A moment ago, one was trying to understand. Now interest shifts to what is animating one's body sitting here:

"We are in a process to come under another influence. There is 'my' attention, secondary attention, that runs up the mountain, sees obstacles, does this or that. If it is 'my' attention, it is not this other Attention which *transforms*. The stream of Attention is there. Be touched by it, link with it, something real in you. Not ideas, thoughts, techniques, not the head, but *that touch*. All my thoughts, feelings, ideas are nothing compared to this precious treasure, this quality of energy that is not mine but what I AM."

PROVENCE, 2007

Sitting on a bench in the garden on a warm July afternoon, watching for Jean-Claude. A striking figure appears by the snack table. He wears a white collared shirt and Oriental overshirt with the front loop-ties left open. Later, introduce myself and hand him the manuscript.

A day passes with not a word. At meals, though, something very curious: when Jean-Claude speaks, there are certain phrases—it's just like hearing Michel.

The next day, sitting outside at a long table with others, manuscript forgotten, happy just to cut vegetables. Nothing is wanted. It is precisely at this moment that the summons comes. Get pad and pen. Climb the stairs to Jean-Claude's office. Heart pounding.

A sunny room with windows all around. Framed photo of Michel. Right away Jean-Claude surprises me when he says, "I hope you don't think the things I've been saying are copying what's in the book." Instant relief! We talk about plans for the book's future.

Mid-week, after listening to people's difficulties, Jean-Claude assembles us outside. We form a long chain to move stones from one location to another. Silently we pass rocks from hand to hand. Bodies turn right, left, right, left, taking on a rhythm. Something about being in that chain…. We are companions together in pure attention.

That afternoon a small group meets with Jean-Claude under a tree. Blue sky. Scent of rosemary. The hum of insects. He says, "I always hear silence in the crickets." And then: "There is a secret consciousness contained in the silence, hidden from ordinary mind. Recognize what is there—I AM—this life-energy coming into me. This tree… when I am quiet in myself, and I look at this tree," here he smiles, "we are already in Paradise."

At dinner he speaks of "an original state for human beings: active attention in the mind, a sensitive body, vibrating feeling." He adds, "This is normal man. This is conscious man. But something must come from me— intensity of attention, capacity to stay."

The final night celebration in the dining hall. Some of us perform funny skits we wrote satirizing the week. So much laughter! Feels so free. At the end of the evening, the room becomes still. Jean-Claude raises one hand above the other, fingers cupped, palms facing, as if holding a ball. He turns to the person on his right and passes along this invisible sphere. We watch this precious something moving from person to person with full care. The room fills with attention. A sacred space. We are One.

Departure morning. In the garden, sitting with Jean-Claude, can't help but mention how noticeable it is, this lightness in how people go about their day, talk with each other.

Jean-Claude says, "This is normal man."

HOLLAND, 2008

Fourteen months later, the invitation comes to bring the full draft of the Michel book to a weeklong retreat in Holland. Cold September. Flat fields spread wide. Jean-Claude is delayed until late that night. He is accompanied by stage-and-screen director Peter Brook, his close associate in Paris at the *Institut G.I. Gurdjieff*.

The communal breakfast is in the dining-hall-in-the-round under a thatched roof. Jean-Claude takes his first look at us. "Like pieces of a puzzle that need to fit together." When people voice frustration, Jean-Claude says, "This morning, words are flowing out like water from a faucet. Must not keep talking like that. We are at the beginning of a process. A fragile process. To be aware of a current."

Unsettled weather. An afternoon reading from *In Search of the Miraculous* (p. 151, Ch. 8, NY 1976) is about identification, the involuntary making of an identity ("me") out of everything that happens—thoughts, feelings, beliefs. Gurdjieff says, "Freedom is first of all freedom from identification…. To learn not to identify, man must first of all not be identified with himself." When is it ever not about me?

Unrelenting rain. A tense lunchtime discussion. Dueling beliefs/identities. Everything in the chicken soup except the chicken?

Jean-Claude says, "There is no problem with the higher consciousness. It is always there. But it is blocked. The space is always occupied by beliefs, thoughts, emotions; protecting my image of myself. Beliefs are of no use. Only this active awareness."

Can the energy animating my body become more important than my thought?

"Direct perception instantly bypasses all the old channels," Jean-Claude continues. "True silence: silence of the mind. Receptive to a finer material, this force, which requires an activation of consciousness. A mobilization again and again. The rest is ideas, philosophy. Mr. Gurdjieff was a very smart man. He put out the bait, but the bait has poison in it."

The room becomes still. Sensitive ears in the silence. When people speak again, all that is personal has dropped away. Miraculously, it's a non-reactive space. In this space, war goes away.

Peter Brook says, "We have become experts in *what isn't*. Now we begin to see *what is*. And everything is different."

After lunch, all of us gather in the living room to watch Part Two of Jean-Claude's documentary *The Seekers of Truth: The Influence of a Master*, including interviews with Gurdjieff's students. Suddenly on screen—Michel. Brings tears. And the wish to *be*.

In the dining hall before dinner, quiet talk among us. Jean-Claude walks in, stops. With a smile, he says, "Something is rising. Like the stock market. Will it go up? How high?" On the last morning, at the departure breakfast, Jean-Claude concludes, "Respect this force appearing. Love it. When one recognizes the force is there, it shows one's work is a reality."

Packing up to go home. Told that Jean-Claude wants to see me. In a little room at the back of the house, even before we sit down, he asks, "Do you have a title for the book?"

"The Next Attention."

"The next attention now," he instantly gets the point. We talk for half an hour. As in Provence, he makes no edits. He offers only a single comment about Michel himself that helps me see better what is necessary and what is not.

In 2010 the book is published under the title *Notes on The Next Attention*.

NEW YORK, 2018

"With a quiet mind, clear, no thoughts, the subtle energy is there," says Jean-Claude during a visit to the Gurdjieff Foundation. He speaks of a kind of reorganization in oneself that comes when there is "a penetration of sacred energy." It requires "a very active attention, watchful for something very high from a different level: a radiance that touches everything."

Can we become sensitive to a Life in us of another quality?

A schedule is posted for group meetings with Jean-Claude or Peter Brook. When not in a meeting, prepare food; set up the dining tables. Mobilize intensely in front of another.

"I need to come every second to a deep, strong contact with this Intelligence. Submit to it, let it penetrate you," says Jean-Claude.

"…Always it's about quality of effort. From that, quantity will come. If the quality is not there, mind goes back to yesterday's memories, imagination, psychology—but am I present now?"

At the day's final meeting, Peter Brook frames for us the future of a living Work. "This is a moment to wash clean of all ideas of Work. This is a new era for Work. Not ideas or beliefs, words. We must embody the finer energy. There is nothing else."

A microphone gets passed to whoever wishes to say something. Behind the words, a shared aligning in attention. Consciousness comes blazing up. A quality flowing through whose very nature is all-loving, all-accepting. Is this the new era? Being Attention. Pure awareness. Loosens the grip of identification. When situated in this animating energy, don't have to make a *me* out of everything that happens.

"Presence is the teacher. Direct experience is all," Jean-Claude ends the work day. "Human beings are the only life forms that can bring this energy of creation to the earth. There is a sacred force, and more and more, you can recognize it. Like the sun coming out.

Affects others. Helps the community. We must embody the subtle energy and bring it into manifestations."

"...It is the most important thing, to stay, silent mind, and just receive. There is nothing I have to do except stay quiet, in contact. Like sitting on the edge of a cliff overlooking the vast emptiness. Stay on that edge."

Soft eyes. Heart open. Gather belongings and go out into the street. Keep something of this inner life alive; conscious attention can come into the world.

Michel's statement from long ago rings true. "This Attention is always there. As we become quieter, steadier in attention, can taste that, can draw nearer. And then suddenly, I am living in awareness of this finer energy, and everything is okay. I can *be*. I can be related to others."

Parting words from Jean-Claude:

Silent mind. No thoughts, no judgments.
Just this Intelligence. So precious.
Present here, receiving impressions.
Deep contact with the Source.

Silence is in me, no matter what.
Knowledge is in the silence.
Nothing that you know will help you.
In silence you will know.

Allow the force of Life to come through.
Embody this force consciously. That is all.

PART ONE

Provence, 2007

There must be real contact with this
Intelligence, this vibration. I don't have to
do anything but be with it.

This stream of energy is eternal, all
around. I just do not perceive it but can
learn to perceive it so it can flow through
me more and more. And this is Work,
and this is all of it, what I am here for.

It is powerful—nuclear—solar.
If I can stay, all is given.

                        —Jean-Claude Lubtchansky

Opening to Presence

There is a Life in you. You can become sensitive, receptive to a finer material. It is important to mobilize attention and to be very watchful. What is needed is a very active attention, a strong attention.

Seeing at each moment: not so easy when talking or moving, but something sees how I am. Then it becomes possible for Attention to flow through.

A level of intensity can come by opening again and again to Presence. If I am near, I go deeper into that dimension. If I am far away, I come back.

Experience it, embody it. It is always there. Be aware of this finer Intelligence coming into me, through me.

All My Beliefs Are Nothing

I do not need to "get something." That is not it. Not something in the future. But the process of opening to the Attention now.

Must respect this finer Intelligence, aware of it. We have the structure to receive it. And then can respect it in others—sacred community—caring for this common treasure.

Must respect that in myself, in others, not demanding, not pushing. Consciousness in everything.

Something needs to be trained to stay. When I can stay, the force of this watchfulness, this Intelligence, has authority. The body, mind, feelings submit. There is unity.

All my ideas, beliefs, about Work are nothing. It is all just ordinary mind, not what *transforms*.

It doesn't matter where you are. Now is all there is. If I am here in the Now, I can be that again.

Life Energy Coming into Me

The natural force of Consciousness can work its process in me. I don't have to "do" anything. Just recognize.

It is a relief not to have to "do" anything.

The body relaxes....

From just above the head, a fine material comes in with breathing... and circulates through the whole body. I... AM....

Recognize what is there, this life energy coming into me. It is always given but not received. We are occupied. The line is busy.

Once I have a taste of this life force through me and all around me, I am responsible to pay attention to That.

What Comes First: Being Present Now

The silence in you, in me—recognizing it, attending to it.

Without criticism, without judgment, of myself, of others. Can receive impressions. Very rich. Is food.

I have a habit of speaking from ordinary mind, analyzing what happened earlier. But the important thing, what comes first, is being present now. Then let words come.

There is a great misunderstanding in the Work: ideas, analysis—this is not Work. Not for one second.

Work begins at the limit—when I can stay.

We abandon before the limit. But now, just to be seen.

The Greatest Help of All

The secret the devil told the seeker: Your passivity is your greatest reminder. When I see it, accept it, the "yes" will appear. Awareness will appear.

The "yes" and the "no"—two forces—are inseparable. *Seeing* and ordinary mind.

There is no problem with ordinary mind except that it cannot work.

The greatest help of all is our passivity because it is a reminder—a shock when I see that I have been asleep. It is the call to wake up. To see the reality of what is, to see the truth.

Every stick has two ends. The "yes" and the "no" are forces that go together. No force is alone.

Cannot prefer one over another like a child—"Which do you prefer, your mother or father?" Necessary to have both forces.

The higher consciousness is always there, ready, waiting to come down. But it is blocked—the space is always occupied by beliefs, thoughts.

Just be seen. Purer *seeing*. Not the ordinary mind—"sense this, sense that"—directing. But being seen. Staying present. Receiving these impressions of myself—whatever it is.

If I could be an empty space—not full of thoughts, feelings—the Goodness would rush in.

An Intelligence Can Permeate

Let it be. See it. Accept as it is. Not to go against but to come toward.

Concentration. And relaxation. The body relaxes.

I am aware of this verticality from the base of the spine up to the head.
Sensitivity.

A fine material comes in with breathing, filling the head, circulating through the whole body.

Breathing becomes more normal.

An Intelligence can permeate.

I... AM....

Like a Tsunami That Washes Away Everything

Sittings are an exercise, not your ticket to heaven. Not "doing an exercise" but we are being exercised.

There is a danger in the Work now about sittings. You sit, "do" an exercise—then go about as usual. Like church on Sunday.

Work means something is given. Work comes from Above, not from myself.

There is an axis of attention in you—but you are not the center of the world.

When this force appears, it is like a tsunami, like a wave that washes away everything else—thoughts, feelings, reactions, ego, washed away in the moment.

This force of Life contains everything, but it needs me to have an influence on the earth. I am here to recognize it, let it pass.

I don't "do" it, but without me it cannot be done.

Open to this life force, always here. To help, to go with life, not against it. While inwardly to remain free.

The only sincerity is with oneself with Presence.

Trust This Awareness

Why a group? Out of the necessity to share a vibration. When this awareness appears, and I know it, all the parts naturally submit. I can trust this awareness, stay in awareness, receive impressions, and attend to Presence.

To awake—
     To die—
          To be reborn—

Not a progression over time, as ordinary mind would have it. But each time I awaken, each time I *see*, I die to that passive part that keeps me a slave and am reborn into Consciousness. Each moment, all at the same time.

"To awake, to die, to be reborn" means all at once. Now.

The Teaching Comes from Within

Am I responsible for the Work in the world?

If I feel that, I must be vigilant, to return to this active reception, to stay, to receive.

I must be determined to wake up. Otherwise it evaporates like water in the desert. I need to be available. To return.

With a real teaching from the Source, there are no teachers. Yes, some are companions on the road. There can be mutual teaching— whoever speaks.

Order comes from the Source. Disorder from the lack of attention. Feeling the lack, you are in front of the truth.

The teaching comes from within. It washes away everything.

If it is "me" and "the world," you suffer because that is not real. The magic wand is acceptance—see it, let it be. Open to this life force, always here.

Yes, there are thoughts, reactions, ego—to protect itself. I don't understand the role of my functions. See—accept—return.

Accompany all with awareness in which all can exist.

Today: to be firm and adaptable, fluid in this awareness. Stable in this awareness.

A Taste of Freedom

Seeing.... At each moment, in question. Something sees, something between the "higher" (the active force) that calls me and the "lower," the body-thoughts-feelings (the passive force).

If I accept the "lower," however it is, then it becomes possible for Attention to flow through it. Need an active attention, actively seeing, sensing the whole of me, constantly renewed.

Then I can know what man is.

Active force—Attention—is the King. Has authority when it appears. The "lower" part wants to participate, to have its place in That. The mind willingly submits when the Presence is there.

"Weak" attention or "lost" attention or "my" attention only means that the Attention has been mixed with ordinary mind.

Acceptance in *seeing* attracts higher forces. It is the opening that permits higher forces to enter and pass through. But something must come from me. Silence. The fewer words, the better off we are.

Unity in a moment—body, ordinary mind, feelings—permits the relationship with this Attention.

Life can help you to work. You do not need any special conditions.

Just to *see*, renewal of *seeing* and accepting as it is, permits another quality to enter. A taste of the Unknown—not knowing— is freedom.

PART TWO

Holland, 2008

My father always said, "The Work is not for me."
One is disturbed by that thought. But if one tries
to understand it in another way, I mean if we
understand that there is another nature within us
that participates in another dimension—something universal. The Work exists for that nature....
Attention is the element that allows the relation
with that other nature.

—Alexandre de Salzmann

Stay just exactly as I am. Not to run away. To stay
with the impression, to let the impressions come
in. The Attention is non-judgmental. Let it touch
your state. There is an Intelligence in me that can
accept. Like the sun. It doesn't care if an ant is
crawling across the rug. The sun radiates with life.

Being awake in this finer energy is like being in
the shower. "In it" feels completely different.
Everything else, the "I" that thinks, believes, feels
this or that—all identification. There is no you.
Either one is identified with the body or one is in
this flow, the true Self.

—Michel de Salzmann

Now, Sensitivity, In the Silence

Why am I here?
Why come together like this?
To go into the Unknown.

I see that I am always creating a form.

Now.... A sensitivity in the body.
No personal aims.
No personal goals.

Sensing head... spine... solar plexus....
In the silence....

I know that I am here.
I sense that I am here.
I feel that I am here.

A New Way of Being Alive

How to work? It is a renewal of attention, an activation of attention. *Seeing* helps this.

Real work comes in silence. I come face to face with what I am.

We need others—so something can pass. It's as if there is a current that needs to pass through all humanity for each individual cell to light up.

We have double mind:

passive mind—very strong, always gives answers in life; that is the prison; and

silent mind—a mind that does not move.

Only from silent mind can I understand what is needed. It is the Unknown. A whole new way of being alive. Requires something from me: activation. This life energy, always flowing through, would otherwise be lost.

Not through wish but through silence can I begin to understand what is needed.

Abandonment of fears, of ideas. Old mind.

Always in question—Am I?

Return to silent mind. Enter the Unknown.

The Door to Silence

"Lord, Have Mercy." This expression is not a religious sentiment, not a religious feeling. It is a conscious feeling.

Stay with just how I am.
Stay with the feeling state.
Stay with the thoughts.
Not trying anything.

And there begins to be an activation, an intelligence that activates a source of attention in the head.

A natural awareness of breathing....
Up...
Down...
Up...
Down...
As if there is an axis joining the abdomen and the head. This axis is the door to silence.

Breathe in the finer energies through the head ... "Lord"

Breathe out, circulating them through the whole body... "Have Mercy."

Lord... Have Mercy....

Passivity Gives the Impulse To Work

Life helps so long as there is the Look from Above. "I" can never "do" it. "I" can never understand it.

Passivity is what makes it possible to work. It gives the impulse to work. Seeing the poverty—thoughts, feelings: it's the human condition. I must be present to it.

A channel can open, more and more, to allow the force of Life to come through.

I can accept whatever is there, and stay with
That.

There is an unknown part of the brain that
can be activated. It takes concentration.
Again and again and again.

Just stay. Just *be*.

To accept oneself no matter how one is—it
is a very great thing.

Awaken the Attention

There is an attraction to this Attention. I must be active in relation to it.

There is the danger of letting it slip away. I am in front of that danger.

Certain conditions are necessary for this quality to appear that brings hope, makes something possible.

There is also an attraction to the demands of life—quite natural—a force pulling in the opposite direction.

I see the danger, and return, to awaken the attention. So when something happens, and there is a reaction, it is a paper tiger—no bite. Otherwise it's a real tiger. Danger!

Something Completely New, Simple

There are guidebooks about the garden, descriptions of the beauty of the garden— but we are not in the garden. We need attention that is free.

Impressions are food for consciousness.

In a second I can open again to this flowing through of fine energy that is always there. Lightness. Something completely new, simple.

Not to "hold" on to something, frozen.

Direct perception.

Not For Myself But Through Myself

We talk too much, make a mishmash. "First line of work" is a complete misunderstanding. There is no first line of work "for myself." Not for myself but through myself.

When receiving this Intelligence, it is not for me, but for another purpose.

Working with others and receiving impressions of another without filters of judgment, reaction.

I give myself completely to the silence.

Vibration of Life Through the Whole Body

I am aware of a finer material—no words for it—vibration of Life. Through the whole body.

"Sensation" is not a word for it—too coarse.

And I am aware of it, quite naturally.

In both legs... in the back... in the head... in both arms... in the chest... in the abdomen....

The body, like an envelope.

And I begin to see that this vibration can be independent of the body.

Even around and a little outside the body, this finer material can be perceived....

What We Are Made For

There are no teachers. There is a Teaching that comes from Above.

When there is a shared moment of Work between two people, there is mutual teaching.

If I work now, I will work tomorrow. I don't have to worry about tomorrow.

It is a shock sometimes to see how I am. Dead or alive? To see the lack, the poverty. The vulgarity of the ego.

I suffer because I feel the lack, but now I am here—my state has changed—and I am still here, in the axis, in the current.

To receive this current from Above. It is what we are made for.

One can be oneself in this stream, can be more oneself, can be what one is.

Mobilize Attention to Receive This Force

I stay. I see the disquiet in the mind—the state of the feelings—

I stay. The more I come closer to Self, the more I am attracted. It is magnetic.

Thoughts are like clouds going by on a lower level. Behind that: freedom.

Activation of attention.
Sensation of the body appears.
And breathing.

There is a substance in breathing that is loaded with energy that comes in with a very fine attention.

It is important to mobilize attention to receive this force. To awaken the attention. Instantly.

To notice when I am passive—and mobilize.

Create a capacity to receive this force and become stable in it.

Embody This Force Consciously

A man can become sensitive, receptive to a finer material.

One must embody this force consciously. The rest is words.

Breathing in…. Respect this force appearing. Worship it. Love it.

It's all here, everything at every moment.

Not just to *be*…{smiles}…. But to be *vibrating*.

PART THREE

New York, 2015-2018

The attention needs to be free. It needs
to be very strong in order not to be distracted by associations or outer events.
There is an external silence and an inner
silence. With an inner silence a higher
energy can come down from Above, and
I can function, think, speak, from this
Intelligence.

Work is not something you can "do."
The higher energy does the work. One
has to open to it, and allow it to flow, to
penetrate one's being. The most important thing? It is to let the higher energy
manifest in me so that all my functions
serve the Light.

—Jean-Claude Lubtchansky

Finer Energy Can Appear

There is the passive, of the earth, and the subtle, a mystery, unknown, from very high—free from all the influences of earth.

Ordinary intelligence pretends to know. One moment one is in the subtle energy but then it gets mixed with the ordinary, and then it strikes like a knife—an arrogance. See that.

The Work is not for *me*. We have outgrown that.

There can be a very active part in us, from a higher part of the mind. Needs exercising. Again and again.

Stability in movement is the challenge. To stay, without rigidity, is also the challenge.

Either one forgets completely (and the room gets loud), or one says nothing but is in one's thoughts.

Watchfulness. To see what takes me away so I can return. So the finer energy can appear. And not overwhelm.

A radiance that penetrates more and more deeply.

An Attention That Can Stay

We need an attention that can stay. Like reading *Beelzebub* three times—it trains the attention. Some religions have you reading texts for 40 years to train the attention.

Something can be very powerful, very active. Bring it into manifestations.

And if we are manifesting and not touching that stream of finer energy, our manifestations have no meaning. We need to be in both streams. To stay.

At the level of earth, it is forms, reactions, very powerful habits in all three parts, body, mind, feelings.

But with all three parts together: God.

Very Active Concentration

At the level of the earth, everything is passive. Our animal, too, serves the earth. It's natural and necessary. In its passivity, it feeds the earth something. There's a mechanical ecology.

But there is the possibility of a very active concentration that allows the other force, active force, to be recognized.

Like a pyramid, with the different parts separated at the base, but at the point at the top, the energy comes in, relates all the parts, brings unity.

Human beings are the only life forms on earth with the three parts, the only ones that can be the bridge to bring this energy of creation to the earth.

Need all parts here, mind, body, feelings—trusting attention aligned with this Intelligence.

There can be a penetration of the sacred energy, irrigating all my parts. Can embody That so it comes to earth. Ascent and descent at the same time.

When there is Presence, there is active awareness of this sacred energy.

An Act of Creation

Work takes place when one is aware of both forces, the passive and the active. To work, to be in both streams and manifesting in the world, is an act of creation. It is allowing this creative force to come into the world.

This tending to higher energy, so important, our responsibility. To care for it. It is the creative source of the universe.

There is a sacred force, and more and more, you can recognize it.

It is an act of creation to embody it.

It does not belong to you but needs your care.

Allow This Intelligence To Enter

Have this Look upon you. Sense the body. That is the opening for higher part of mind, silent mind, to allow this Intelligence to enter.

The attention is the channel. Strong. Can stay. Brings freedom from body, feelings, thoughts. All of it melts away.

Return to Presence, even to see at that moment when associations or reactions take over. That can be seen. So that this other Intelligence can appear. Need to be present. Otherwise, it's just ideas.

We are made for this, built for this. All that we've experienced of this is there in our subconscious, to be tapped in an instant.

Sensation, sensing the body, is the support for another quality to appear. Submit to it, let it penetrate you.

Be in this "shower."

Return to This Light in You

Return again and again to Presence, this Light in you.

Only with this Light in you can you be a human being, present.

Only with this Light in you can you see more and more what happens—the pull of passivity, of associations, of "denying force" that can awaken an equally strong "affirming force."

You must be in the Light, "in the shower," to *see.* My attention, like a muscle, needs to be strong and steady, to repeat, to stay, so that *seeing* appears, and this Intelligence.

Then I am free, living in another body, the beginning of another body.

And another quality of feeling appears.

Community Can Help

Community helps us. When not "in the shower," I am like everyone else—no different—so not judge myself or others.

Be more objective, knowing that if that Look is upon him or her, everything is okay.

We have two levels. The animal, of the earth: forms, passivity. And what I am.

Need real attention to come under the influence of this other Intelligence, which is on a much grander scale. I need to be watchful.

Conditions of the community can help. What is needed is this Intelligence, an axis in me.

There's the one who pretends to work, pretends to know. The one who orders about all the others. That one must submit to a higher part of the mind—silent mind.

The Group Must Have An Aim

In groups, if the ordinary appears—talk of the past when I had a taste of something, read something—yes, but am I present now?

The group must have an aim, to be fully present to this Intelligence every moment.

If the quality is not there, it becomes bland. If the group has the aim that the ordinary has no place there, then the ordinary must be silent. The functions must submit. Cut down the trees! Come now into a strong contact with this Intelligence.

Let real *I* speak from this Intelligence.

You can transmit only what you yourself embody. You must *be* what you are talking about.

Silent Mind

The quality of effort is all.

In life, too, must be active in front of every situation. It is an education.

Learn how to mobilize attention to allow this contact to appear.

Sensitive.
Open.

Silent mind.

No thoughts, just this Intelligence. The demand to stay with That.

I need to be watchful. Accept the situation and see what is necessary and what is not.

Present—here—receiving impressions.

In life, in groups, the same.
Go inward.

Deep contact with the Source.

Return A Million Times

Consciousness. All my parts here. The body becomes sensitive.

Be watchful. Only when present can I see the pull of the force of passivity—associations—reactions. Then there is a new possibility. Of new life. It's a natural process. We were made for it.

It doesn't stay, this Intelligence, this force animating these forms.

So, I need to return a million times—return to Presence.

A Home in Me for Sacred Intelligence

Our aim in this work is to know myself. I need to be in the Light to know myself. I need to materialize an independent body of consciousness.

The energy is not enough. I need a place in me that can receive the Intelligence, a home in me for this sacred Intelligence coming into me. Then there can be independence, freedom.

Stay in the Light. Without desire to change anything. The tension is there. The resistance is there. Accept it as it is, all of it as it is.

Be kind to it. Let it be. And open.

Open the window. Why stay in the dark?

A Body of Awareness

Resistance and passivity are like a magnet. This other force, of Consciousness, is also like a magnet. I'm easily attracted to reactions, feelings, associations. But this other force can be in me. I can be a channel for That.

Both are there, like pedals on a bicycle. I need resistance for this Consciousness to appear.

But perhaps there is not yet enough material crystallized in me for the Light to stay.

I need to open, to materialize this other body in me so it can receive nourishment, this Intelligence, this sacred force.

An attention is needed, a pure attention. That requires a silent mind, a quiet mind;

then the sensation of the body grows stronger.

The higher energy needs a second body in order to manifest, a body of awareness.

When I see that I am no longer in contact with the awareness, I come back, a thousand times a day.

Trust This Other Energy

I need to be responsible for my state.

There are always going to be reactions—passivity—always there—my functions.

To become responsible is the aim of normal man. To become responsible for one's state.

I can begin to have confidence, to trust this other energy coming through me.

Like a flower, opening to the sun.

Let It Penetrate Deeply

When I have a strong taste of this other energy, I can feel when I go away from it. And I can return.

I need to go away to return, to affirm this other force.

Relaxation of the body.
Impressions coming in.
Quiet mind.

And something appears.

We need to resonate more with this higher vibration. Let it penetrate deeply. When you have a taste of that, you can come back.

Listen As If It Is All Unknown

My situation—thoughts, feelings. A state of reaction, in accord with passivity. Must separate from it—not suppress, but separate. Disengage.

Become deeply related to That which animates the whole of me.

Try now.

Objectivity is needed. Not personal.

A matter of attitude.

Listen as if it is all Unknown.

Objectivity Is Needed in Seeing Myself

We all have the same difficulty. Leave it. Come back to what is essential.

We are not interested in the coarse; we are interested in the subtle. This central axis. All of our interest has to be there!

Go with what is real in me. My life depends on it.

There is no step between the ordinary and the higher. It is not a ladder.

You must see for yourself. You must find out for yourself.

Objectivity is what is needed in seeing myself. Whatever is seen, loses its power.

Then I can disengage, from reaction, from what I'm identified with.

It's all Unknown. Come back to the quiet in you, and sense.

You are faced with a flat tire. You can't just look at it and wish it to be filled. You must fill it.

Tree of Life, Rooted in Attention

There is an active and a passive part of body, of feeling, of mind.

The active part of mind is clear attention; of feeling, this feeling of the sacred; of body, intentional movement.

The passive part of mind is associations; of feeling, reaction; of body, automatism.

Must find your center of gravity in the active parts.

This body materializing in me—it is the Tree of Life. A body of Life. Rooted in attention.

Have This Look Upon You

Passivity is strong. It will always be there.

Passivity is a force that awakens another force.

Need real attention to come under the influence of this other force, this other Intelligence. Must have this Look upon you. Sense the body. Otherwise it's all associations and just repeats and repeats.

When the King is not there, all the servants serve themselves.

When the King is there, all the servants take their proper place and serve the King.

Return, so this other Intelligence can appear.

Come into Presence

The attention is the channel.

Come into our whole Presence.

Feel when you go away, and you can return.

Stay in the Light. Without desire to change anything.

There is nothing I have to do except stay in contact.

It is the most important thing—to stay and just receive. No matter what.

There is the legend of the lame horse who, all of a sudden… sprouts wings!

Something Real in You

This tending to higher energy, so important, our responsibility.

Thinking, dreaming about work—not of any use. Letting go of that habit.

Ordinary mind is powerful. There is arrogance, indifference, tensions. There is this "artificial one" in the way.

Watchfulness. See what takes you away. Come back.

Direct experience is all.

There is a sacred force. It does not belong to you but needs your care. It infuses all of you with Intelligence. It's what we're here for. Recognize it. Trust it. Something real in you.

APPENDIX

Jean-Claude's French Translation of
Michel de Salzmann's Opening Talks
from *Notes on The Next Attention*

We don't need to travel a great distance to pass
between one world and the other. It's so close; it's
like lightning. We can instantly change worlds....

Try to understand what attitude is needed to be
quite lightly related to this way of living.... How
to free my attention so that it can partly remain
in contact and at the same time allow the usual
ordinary manifestations.... Attention that is not
immediately taken.

—Jean-Claude Lubtchansky

So remember this other mode of being, more
sensitive, called to stand in the place that can receive impressions. Instead of my mind-dominated
usual condition, with an active attention something refined can penetrate... deep Intelligence.

Total sensitivity. Total receptivity. A kind of
whole-hearted emptiness. A trusting emptiness.
So that a finer influence can act on me, in the
silence. And even despite myself, I begin to
receive it, yield to it, a channel for it. And perhaps
a threshold is reached when I belong to That.

—Michel de Salzmann

1.

Peut-être n'avons nous pas le désir de nous tourner vers l'intérieur. Observons seulement. Laissons faire. Le pouvoir de l'attention peut produire une énergie se répandant progressivement dans tout le corps. Ce dont j'ai le plus besoin c'est de connaître qui je suis et je peux en faire l'expérience lorsque cette énergie s'incarne dans mon corps.

Tout ce qui est nécessaire pour développer pleinement une présence est ici en nous. Il y a un mouvement qui est sacré, il peut descendre en nous et nous y conduire. Il fait voir les obstacles, pensées et sentiments, entraînant une pression qui nous éloigne de cette présence. Mais, si je peux laisser cette attention pure m'animer, me relâcher intérieurement et simplement rester avec ce processus, je peux alors rejoindre d'une manière naturelle ce que je suis.

L'attention est une énergie sacrée qui me pénètre. Il faut être sensible à sa présence et la reconnaître encore et encore.

2.

Il s'agit de laisser l'expérience se faire sans avoir d'idées préconçues à son sujet, de trouver sa place dans un espace silencieux et de reconnaître organiquement ce que signifie être présent, afin de pouvoir y revenir.

Pendant des années, nous avons voulu nous aider de différents moyens, mais par moments, il y a assez d'énergie disponible pour qu'apparaissent une sensibilité, puis que survienne une intelligence. Cela ne provient pas des moyens, mais de laisser être sans rien changer et de s'ouvrir à l'attention.

Plus l'attention se renforce, plus le corps s'allège, mais cette impression agréable n'est pas le plus important, c'est l'attention qui vient en premier, le corps en second.

Je suis effectivement pris par toutes sortes de contradictions, mais j'ai un tel désir de me joindre à cette énergie que plus rien d'autre ne compte.

3.

L'essentiel est de rechercher la conscience en devenant réceptif à une attention plus pure, plus libre, seule matière permettant de recevoir des influences plus fines.

Quand cette intelligence de la conscience apparaît, ne pas la trahir, la respecter. Elle est là, très proche, c'est moi qui en suis loin. Si je suis pris, c'est parce que je me suis centré sur moi-même, sur mes fonctions, que je suis entraîné par mes pensées, mes sentiments et toutes mes réactions. Je dois reconnaître avec remord que je trahis cette intelligence, le voir, car ce que je ne respecte pas va disparaître. L'attention ne doit pas être prise, elle doit rester libre des associations habituelles. Elle est ce qui relie le niveau supérieur à l'inférieur, mais elle a besoin de ce sol ferme qu'est le corps.

La sensation est toujours le résultat de la rencontre de deux forces. Elle provient d'un contact entre l'attention et le corps, elle n'est pas le but, elle est comme un terrain où l'attention peut se maintenir. Elle est en moi un axe vivant dans une myriade de mouvements.

Un sentiment naît de la fusion du corps, de la pensée et de l'âme. La respiration aide à rejoindre cet axe, à le sentir, à faire l'expérience directe de la totalité de soi-même.

Il apparaît alors une attention participant à un mouvement plus grand que nous, dont nous ne sommes qu'une partie.

4.

Comment ne pas aimer ce qui pénètre en moi et ne pas désirer s'y accorder?

Tout est amour.

Comment correspondre à cette attention sacré ? Quand je suis relié à cette intelligence, je la respecte comme témoin de la Source, elle peut avoir une action dans le monde.

Tout commence avec l'impression que j'ai de moi-même. Non au moyen d'une idée théorique à propos de la sincérité, mais par une interrogation profonde. Puis-je parvenir à cette évidence ?

Le moi n'est alors plus à la même place, je peux écouter, recevoir les impressions. Il ne s'agit pas d'une manipulation psychologique, il ne s'agit pas d'y penser et de croire que je peux le faire.

Cette attention est dans le corps et au-delà du corps, ce n'est pas vous qui l'avez créée. Mais prenant en compte cette intelligence, vous pouvez irrésistiblement y correspondre et la rejoindre.

Original in English:
Dr. Michel de Salzmann's talks, from *Notes on The Next Attention* (hardcover, 2010) and *The Next Attention* (paperback, 2023).

Note that English was a second language for Michel. Quoted material is faithful to his English, never paraphrased, in hopes of conveying its "energetical" quality.

1.

Perhaps there is no inclination to turn inward. Let it be. Just watch. The power of attention more and more can fill the body. The greatest need we have is to know who I am, and I can know that only by this energy incarnating the body.

Everything we need is here in us. Everything for fuller being. There is a kind of sacred descent of attention that can bring this about. Seeing the obstacles, thoughts, feelings, yes, perhaps a pressure that keeps me from it. But if I can relax inside, just allow the pure attention to flow in, be in that. Very natural. It's what we are.

Attention: a sacred energy coming into me. Be sensitive to it. Recognize again and again that it is there.

2.

To let the experience open—not to be too quick to have ideas about it. Situate yourself in this calm, empty space.

Know in your body what it is to be present so you can find it again.

For many years we try methods, but then, at moments, there is enough energy for a sensitivity to appear and then for this Intelligence to appear. It is not the methods that produce it. It's letting everything be, inside, just as it is, and opening to the attention.

The stronger the attention, the lighter the body. Very pleasant—yes—but not to be taken by this lightness. The attention is coming first, the body second.

Pushes and pulls here and there maybe, but I am so attracted to be joined with this energy, there is nothing else as important. That is how it feels.

3.

Searching for consciousness—that is the essential. You are too much concentrated on yourself. Searching for consciousness, sensitive, receiving with an attention more and more free, more and more pure.

And when this central Intelligence appears, to respect it, more and more. Not to betray it.

It is very near, but we are far away. To realize, with remorse, that I have been coarse, have betrayed it. So now, to recognize that, to see.

Attention is the only matter that can receive finer influences. Free attention— not taken by anything. If taken, it means I am concentrated on me, my functions, a thought, a feeling, a reaction. Free attention: an attention that is free of the vibrations on the surface.

Attention is what relates the higher and lower. But it is not free—taken mostly by thoughts. It needs a ground: the body.

"Sensation"—always the result of the meeting of two forces. Sensation is the experience of contact between attention and body, not for itself, but as a ground so the attention can stay.

A living axis in me, among the myriad of movements. I can be sensitive to them, sensitive to breathing.

And a feeling arises of body, mind, and soul here together.

How important breathing is. It helps you join the axis. To have a direct experience of all of myself, a central attention.

Participating in a movement greater than ourselves, of which all of this is part.

4.

How can one help but love that which enters, all goodness, and wish to correspond to That?

Love is one aspect of it.

See how to correspond to this sacred Attention coming into me. When I am related to this Intelligence, respect it as the representative of the sacred, from the Source; then it can have an action in the world.

Everything begins with the impression of myself. Not some theoretical idea about sincerity, but deep questioning. Can I come to this evidence?

Then I'm not thinking about me but can listen, can receive impressions of the other, called to stand in the place that can receive impressions. Not psychological—not thinking about it, imagination about it.

This Attention is in the body and beyond the body. "You" cannot "do" it—fortunately. But recognizing this Intelligence, you can correspond to it, and then join it, irresistibly.

∾

Nothing belongs to me except that
which recognizes my true nature.

Can I liberate myself from all my
concerns and enter the mystery?
For this I need free attention.

The true nature of attention is
that it is multidimensional. It can
know its nature only when it is
free of "commitments." Quiet
mind. Just receiving impressions.

And even subtler energies can
come in... the Light can come in....
This attention in me can know
its Source.

—Michel de Salzmann

CODA

Can I be in contact with that in me that recognizes a Life in me of another quality?

I need to be in the Light to know myself.

Silent mind. No thoughts, no judgments, just this Intelligence. I don't have to do anything but be with it.

Accept the situation and see what is necessary and what is not.

Present here, receiving impressions. Deep contact with the Source.

I can begin to have confidence, to trust this other energy coming through me.

It is like a flower, opening to the sun.

Have this Look upon you. Sense the body. That is the opening for higher part of mind—silent mind—to allow this Intelligence to enter.

Consciousness is without limit—so expansive, so immense.

Work is on cosmic scale. Work is not something you can "do." The higher energy does the work. Open to it.

To think about the Work is the greatest sin. It takes me away.

A fine energy exists along with everything else. This vibration can connect you with your work.

You must *be* what you are talking about.

Sensation is a sacred road.

The attention needs to be free in order not to be distracted by associations or events.

Return to presence, even to see at that moment when associations or reactions take over—so this other Intelligence can appear—both joy and suffering there at the same moment.

Objectivity is what is needed in seeing myself. Then I can disengage, from reaction, from what I'm identified with.

Need real attention to come under the influence of this other force, this other Intelligence, which is on a much grander scale. Otherwise, it's all associations and just repeats and repeats.

Silence is in me, no matter what.

With an inner silence a higher energy can come down from above and I can function, think, speak, from this Intelligence.

And another quality of feeling appears.

All that we've experienced of This is there in our subconscious, to be tapped in an instant.

The attention is the channel. Must be like a nail—so strong—must stay.

Freedom from body, feelings, thoughts—all of it melts away.

This other body, finer body, is a support for receiving this Intelligence.

To work is an act of creation. It is allowing this creative force to come into the world.

This tending to higher energy, so important. To trust it. To care for it.

I need to come, every second, to a deep, strong contact with this Intelligence. We were made for it.

The Teaching comes from within. Presence is the teacher.

— Jean-Claude Lubtchansky

Printed in Great Britain
by Amazon

47263179R00069